Phonics for Kindergarten

apple

boat

SHELL EDUCATION

Contributing Authors

Jodene Smith, M.S.

Mary Rosenberg, M.A.Ed.

Suzanne I. Barchers, Ed.D.

Chandra Prough, M.A.Ed.

Christine Dugan, M.A.Ed.

Publishing Credits

Robin Erickson, *Production Director;* Lee Aucoin, *Creative Director;* Timothy J. Bradley, *Illustration Manager*; Sara Johnson, M.S.Ed., *Editorial Director*; Evelyn Garcia, *Editor;* Grace Alba, *Designer;* Corinne Burton, M.A.Ed., *Publisher*

Standards

© 2010 National Governors Association Center for Best Practices and Council of Chief State School Officers (CCSS)

Shell Education

5301 Oceanus Drive
Huntington Beach, CA 92649-1030
http://www.shelleducation.com

ISBN 978-1-4258-1096-2

© 2014 Shell Education Publishing, Inc.

Table of Contents

Developing Foundational Skills in Reading

Foundational Skills: Phonics for Kindergarten has been written with kindergarteners in mind! The pages in this book provide children practice with some of the foundational skills needed to be successful readers—phonics and word recognition.

There has been much written and said about phonics. All the talk has left questions about what phonics is and whether it should be taught. Simply put, phonics is the relationship between letters and sounds. When a child learns that the letter *s* makes the /s/ sound, that is phonics! Since children need to be able to figure out words in order to read, it is important that they understand the relationship between the letters that are on the page and the sounds these letters make (Chall 1995).

There has been much research to show that phonics needs to be explicitly taught and included in good reading programs. In fact, the National Reading Panel (2000) included phonics as one of the five essential components of reading instruction. The fact is that a large number of words in English do follow patterns and rules. Instruction and practice with phonics gives children an opportunity to develop their understanding of the relationship between letters and sounds. Additionally, researchers have found that phonic awareness is a strong predictor of later reading achievement (Juel 1988; Griffith and Olson 1992; Lomax and McGee 1987; Tunmer and Nesdale 1985).

But not all words can be figured out with phonics (Cook 2004). For example, the words *of* and *the* cannot be sounded out with knowledge of letter and sound relationships. There are several word lists that have been compiled of words that occur in print with high frequency, and many of these words do not follow patterns and rules (Fry and Kress 2006). Children need to know other ways to read or figure out words that they cannot apply phonics to, such as recognizing words by sight or using context. For this reason, practice with frequently occurring grade-level-appropriate sight words is an important component of reading.

This book provides children with many opportunities to practice key skills in both phonics and word recognition. Practicing these skills help build the foundation for successful readers. And although the traditional saying is "practice makes perfect," a better saying for this book is "practice makes successful readers."

Understanding the Standards

The Common Core State Standards were developed through the Common Core State Standards Initiative. The standards have been adopted by many states in an effort to create a clear and consistent framework and to prepare students for higher education and the workforce. The standards were developed as educators worked together to incorporate the most effective models from around the country and globe, to provide teachers and parents with a shared understanding of what students are expected to learn at each grade level, and as a continuum throughout the grades. Whereas previously used state-developed standards showed much diversity in what was covered at each grade level, the consistency of the Common Core State Standards provides educators a common understanding of what should be covered at each grade level and to what depth.

The Common Core State Standards have the following qualities:

- They are aligned with college and work expectations.

- They are clear, understandable, and consistent.

- They include rigorous content and application of knowledge through high-order skills.

- They build upon strengths and lessons of current state standards.

- They are informed by other top-performing countries so that all students are prepared to succeed in our global economy and society.

- They are evidence based.

Students who meet these standards within their K–12 educations should have the skills and knowledge necessary to succeed in their educational careers and beyond.

Getting Started

Practicing the phonics skills targeted in this book gives children the foundation they need to become better readers. It is because you realize this that you have purchased this book! Following are some tips for using this book:

- Set aside a specific time of day to work on the activities found in this book. This will establish consistency.

- Emphasize completing only a couple of pages each time the child works in the book rather than lots of activity pages at one time.

- Keep all practice sessions positive and constructive. If the mood becomes tense or if you and the child get frustrated, set the activities aside and look for another time for the child to practice.

- Help with instructions, if necessary. If the child is having difficulty understanding what to do, talk through some of the problems with him or her.

- Use the answer key provided on pages 88–94. Once the desired number of pages have been completed, help check the work. If possible, take time to go back and correct any problems missed. Immediately reviewing errors with the help of an adult helps children learn from their mistakes.

Making It Work

Understanding the key features of this book will help you effectively use it as you work with the child to develop and practice reading skills. Following are some features of the book that will help you.

- **Standards-based practice.** The exercises in *Foundational Skills: Phonics for Kindergarten* are aligned with the Common Core State Standards. Each activity page focuses on a particular concept, skill, or skill set and provides students opportunities to practice and achieve mastery.

- **Clear, easy-to-understand activities.** The exercises in this book are written in a user-friendly style.

- **Stand-alone activity pages.** Each activity is flexible and can be used independently.

- **Concise number of exercises.** The number of exercises on each page is limited to six. Children feel more comfortable and confident in attempting a page when the number of exercises is not overwhelming to them.

The chart below provides suggestions for how to implement the activities.

Preteaching	Reteaching
Choose pages with concepts the child has not yet learned. This will take some teaching on your part in order to help the child understand the concept, so be sure you are comfortable and prepared to explain the new concept.	Use pages related to concepts the child has struggled with in school or while doing homework. If there are any areas or specific standards with which the child may need some additional instruction and practice, use the Standards Correlation Chart on page 9 to help locate pages that will be useful.
Practice	**Review**
Select pages that are consistent with what is being taught in school. By providing additional practice with those reading concepts, you will help the child master them more quickly.	Choose pages with concepts the child may have learned earlier in the school year. By reviewing previously taught concepts, the child will benefit from refreshing those skills.

Correlations to Standards

Shell Education is committed to producing educational materials that are research- and standards-based. In this effort, we have correlated all of our products to the academic standards of all 50 United States, the District of Columbia, the Department of Defense Dependent Schools, and all Canadian provinces. We have also correlated to the Common Core State Standards.

How to Find Standards Correlations

To print a customized correlation report of this product for your state, visit our website at **http://www.shelleducation.com** and follow the on-screen directions. If you require assistance in printing correlation reports, please contact Customer Service at 1-877-777-3450.

Purpose and Intent of Standards

Legislation mandates that all states adopt academic standards that identify the skills students will learn in kindergarten through grade twelve. Many states also have standards for pre-K. This same legislation sets requirements to ensure the standards are detailed and comprehensive.

Standards are designed to focus instruction and guide adoption of curricula. Standards are statements that describe the criteria necessary for students to meet specific academic goals. They define the knowledge, skills, and content students should acquire at each level. Standards are also used to develop standardized tests to evaluate students' academic progress. Teachers are required to demonstrate how their lessons meet state standards. State standards are used in the development of all of our products, so educators can be assured they meet the academic requirements of each state.

Common Core State Standards

The lessons in this book are aligned to the Common Core State Standards (CCSS). The standards listed on page 9 support the objectives presented throughout the lessons.

Correlations to Standards

Skill	Pages
Demonstrate basic knowledge of one-to-one letter-sound correspondences by producing the primary sound or many of the most frequent sounds for each consonant.	11, 13–19, 21–27, 29–39, 41–51, 53–62
Associate the long and short sounds with common spellings (graphemes) for the five major vowels.	63–72
Isolate and pronounce the initial, medial vowel, and final sounds (phonemes) in three-phoneme (consonant-vowel-consonant) words.	12, 20, 28, 40, 52
Read common high-frequency words by sight.	73–78

Letter Formation Guide

Name: _____ **Date:** _____

Directions: Trace and write the letter *Aa*.

Directions: Find and color all of the *a*'s.

Primary Sound *a*

Name: _____ **Date:** _____

Directions: Write the missing *a*'s. Color the pictures.

1.

h _ _ _ _ t

2.

m _ _ _ _ p

3.

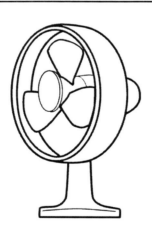

f _ _ _ _ n

4.

r _ _ _ _ t

Name: _____ **Date:** _____

Directions: Trace and write the letter *Bb*.

Directions: Find and color all of the *b*'s.

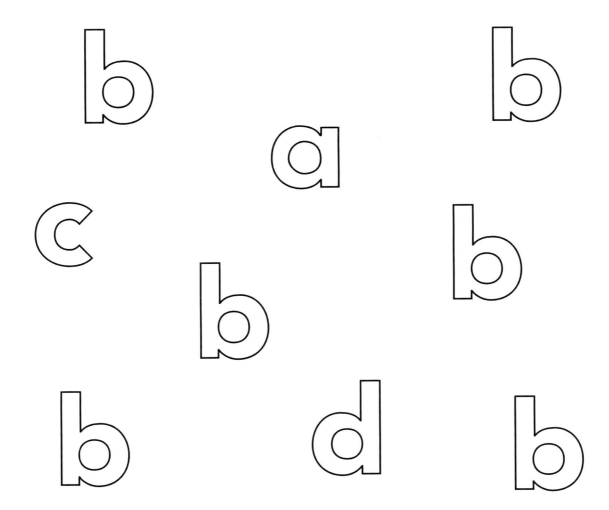

Primary Sound *b*

Name: _____ **Date:** _____

Directions: Name each picture below. Write the missing *b*'s. Then read the sentences.

1.

I see a __b__ear.

2.

I see a ____ed.

3.

I see a
__utterfly__.

4.

I see a ____oat.

Name: _____ **Date:** _____

Directions: Trace and write the letter *Cc*.

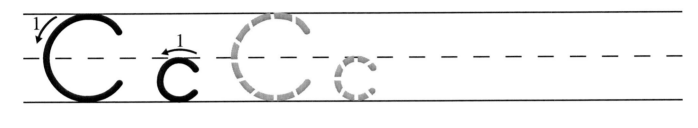

Directions: Match each capital *C* to its lowercase *c*.

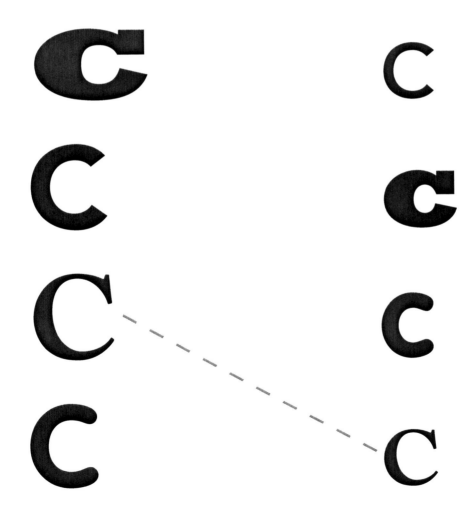

Primary Sound *c*

Name: _____ **Date:** _____

Directions: Name each picture below. Draw a line to match the pictures that go together.

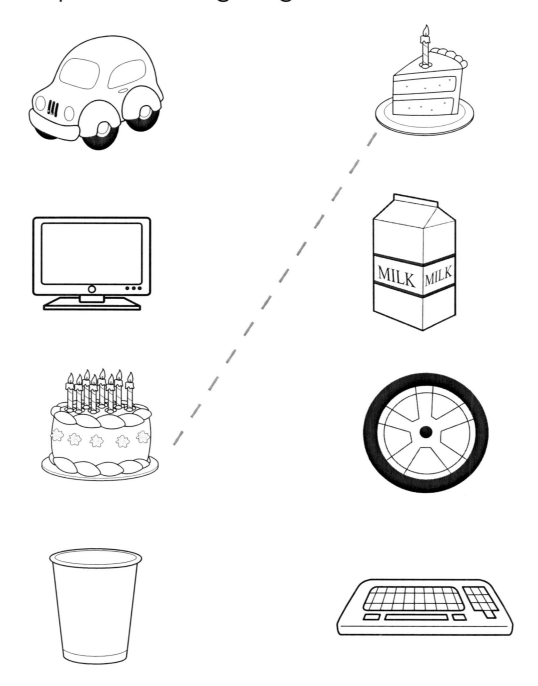

Name: _____ **Date:** _____

Directions: Trace and write the letter *Dd*.

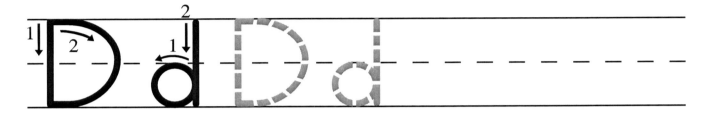

Directions: Look at the letters below. Find and color the boxes that have *d*'s in them. What did you make?

v	c	e	d	f	b	c	d	u
r	s	t	d	g	e	s	d	i
o	d	d	d	h	d	d	d	y
n	d	u	d	i	d	r	d	r
m	d	d	d	j	d	d	d	f

Primary Sound *d*

Name: _____**Date:** _____

Directions: Name each picture below. Color the pictures that begin with *d*.

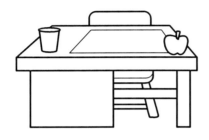

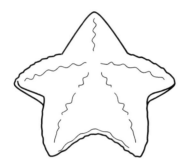

Directions: Find and color the boxes that have *d*'s in them.

1.

d	m	c
h	d	k
l	e	d

2.

f	i	y
d	d	d
n	e	j

Name: _____ **Date:** _____

Directions: Trace and write the letter *Ee*.

Directions: Find and color all of the *e*'s.

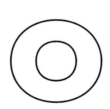

Primary Sound *e*

Name: _____ **Date:** _____

Directions: Write the missing *e*'s. Color the pictures.

1.	2.
 n _____ t	 t _____ n
3.	4.
 p _____ n	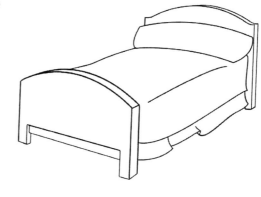 b _____ d

Name: _____ **Date:** _____

Directions: Trace and write the letter *Ff*.

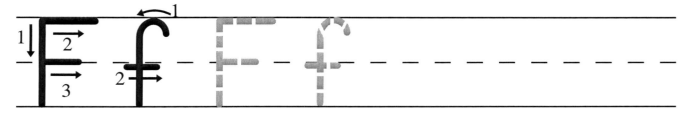

Directions: Look at the letters below. Find and color the boxes that have *f*'s in them. What did you make?

f	f	f	t	x	f	f	f
f	b	j	u	r	f	z	r
f	f	n	c	f	f	f	q
f	h	k	v	w	f	o	p
f	g	l	m	n	f	m	d

Primary Sound *f*

Name: _____ **Date:** _____

Directions: Name each picture below. Write the letter *f* under each picture that begins with the letter *f*.

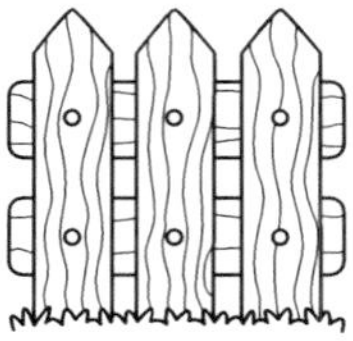

1. _____	2. _____
3. _____	4. _____
5. _____	6. _____
7. _____	8. _____

Name: _____ **Date:** _____

Directions: Trace and write the letter *Gg*.

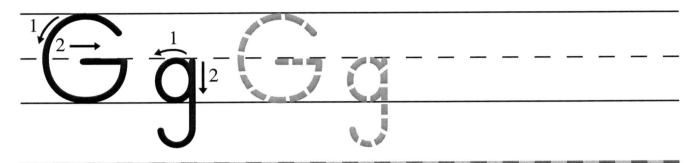

Directions: Find and color the boxes that have *g*'s in them.

1.

a	r	g
o	g	m
g	w	c

2.

g	c	s
n	g	e
y	r	g

3.

n	g	v
m	g	u
l	g	k

4.

g	g	g
t	s	f
j	i	h

Primary Sound *g*

Name: _____ **Date:** _____

Directions: Name each picture below. Write the missing *g*'s. Then color the pictures.

1. game	2. ift
3. oat	4. uitar
5. orilla	6. irl

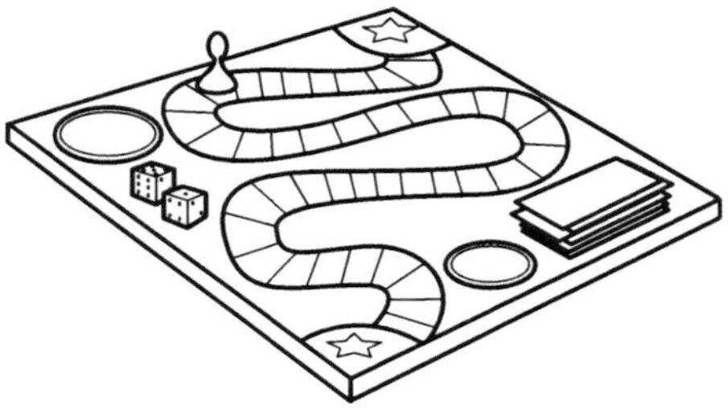

Name: _____ **Date:** _____

Directions: Trace and write the letter *Hh*.

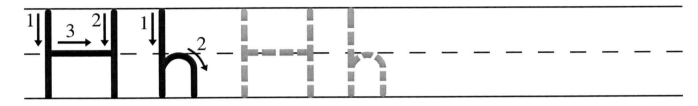

Directions: Find and color all of the *h*'s.

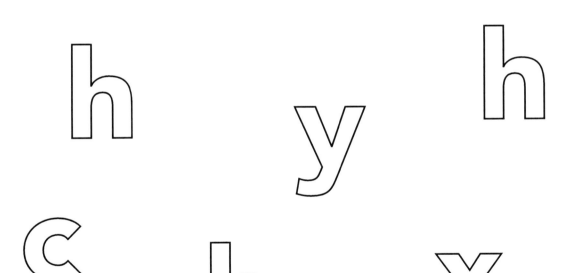

Primary Sound *h*

Name: _____ Date: _____

Directions: Name each picture below. Write the missing *h*'s. Then color the pictures.

1. h orse	2. ____ ouse
3. ____ ose	4. ____ ammer
5. ____ eart	6. ____ anger

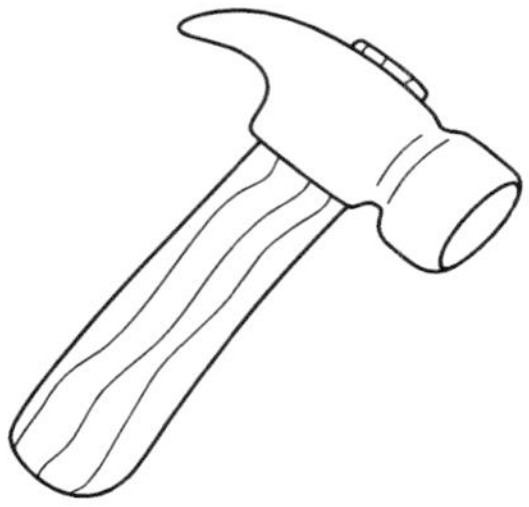

Name: _____ **Date:** _____

Directions: Trace and write the letter *Ii*.

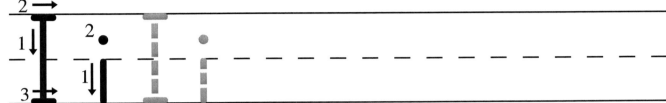

Directions: Find and color all of the *i*'s.

   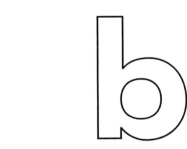

 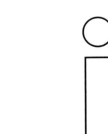 

Primary Sound *i*

Name: _____ **Date:** _____

Directions: Write the missing i's. Color the pictures.

1.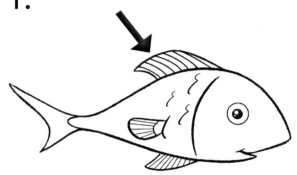

f _____ n

2.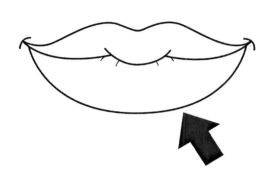

l _____ p

3.

w _____ g

4.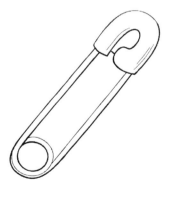

p _____ n

Name: _____ **Date:** _____

Directions: Trace and write the letter *Jj*.

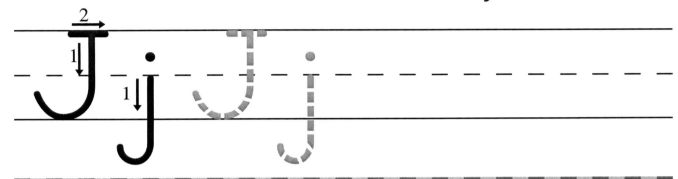

Directions: Name each picture below. Write the missing *j*'s. Then color the pictures.

1.  ar

2. ___ et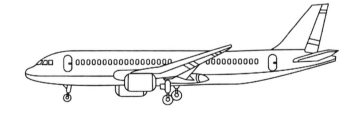

3. ___ ug

Primary Sound *j*

Name: _____**Date:** _____

Directions: Name each picture below. Write the missing *j*'s. Then color the pictures.

1.

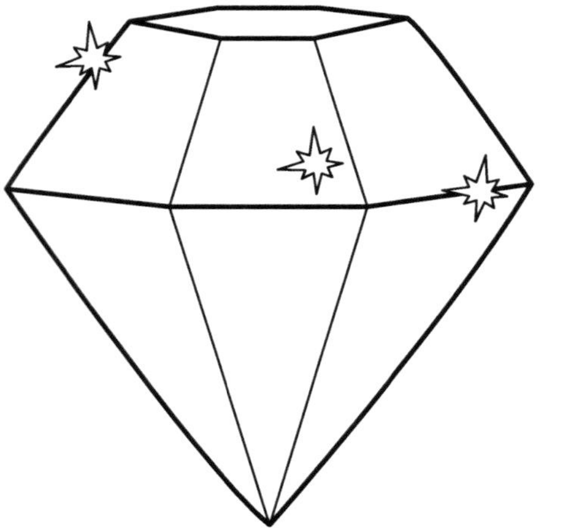

___jewel___

2.

___acket

3.

___ug

4.

___aguar

Name: _____ **Date:** _____

Directions: Trace and write the letter *Kk*.

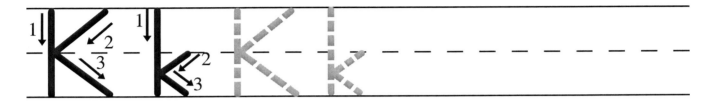

Directions: Find and color the matching *k* in each row.

k	k	k	k
k	k	k	k
k	k	k	k
k	k	k	k

Primary Sound *k*

Name: _____**Date:** _____

Directions: Some of the pictures below begin with *k*. Draw a line from these pictures to the kangaroo. Then color the pictures.

Name: _____ **Date:** _____

Directions: Trace and write the letter *Ll*.

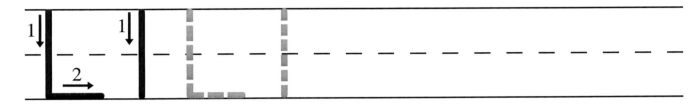

Directions: Find and color all of the *l*'s.

Primary Sound *l*

Name: _____ **Date:** _____

Directions: Some of the pictures below begin with the letter *l.* Draw a line from these pictures to the lizard.

Name: _____ **Date:** _____

Directions: Trace and write the letter *Mm*.

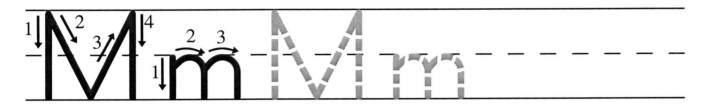

Directions: Find and color all of the *m*'s.

Primary Sound *m*

Name: _____ **Date:** _____

Directions: Name each picture below. Write the missing *m*'s. Then color the pictures.

1. _m_arker	2. ____ouse
3. ____agnet	4. ____onkey
5. ____uffin	6. ____ap

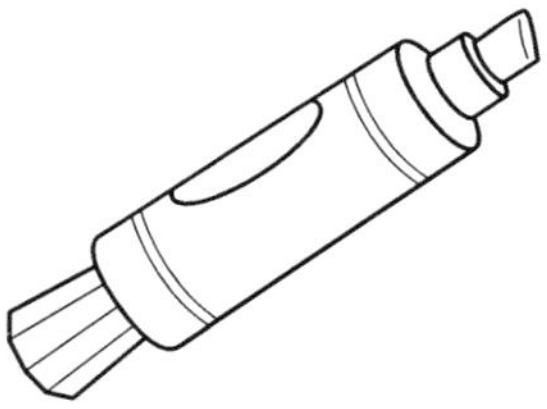

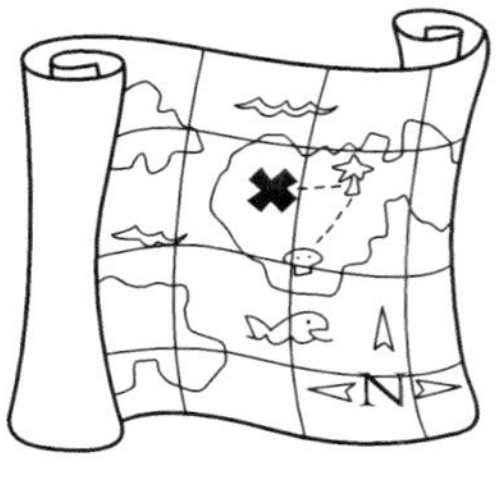

Name: _____ **Date:** _____

Directions: Trace and write the letter *Nn*.

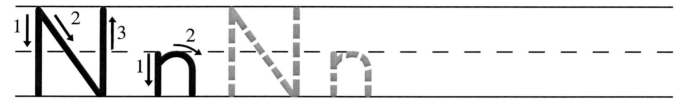

Directions: Name each picture below. Draw a line to match the pictures that go together.

Primary Sound *n*

Name: _____ **Date:** _____

Directions: Look at the picture. Color the things that begin with *n*.

Name: _____ **Date:** _____

Directions: Trace and write the letter *Oo*.

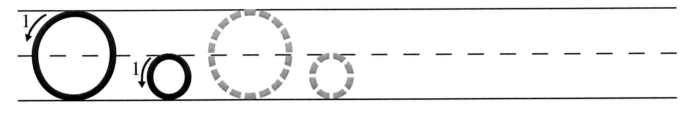

Directions: Find and color all of the *o*'s.

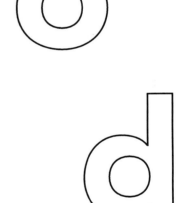

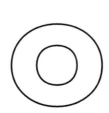

Primary Sound *o*

Name: _____ **Date:** _____

Directions: Write the missing *o*'s. Color the pictures.

1.  c ___ p	**2.**  l ___ g
3. 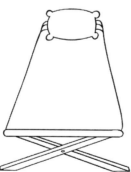 c ___ t	**4.** d ___ t

Primary Sound *p*

Name: _____ **Date:** _____

Directions: Trace and write the letter *Pp*.

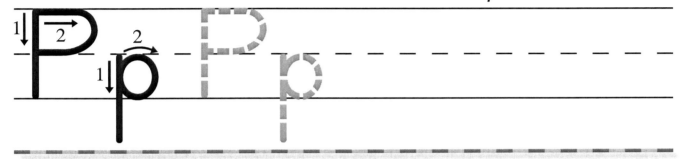

Directions: Name each picture below. Color the pictures that begin with *p*.

Primary Sound *p*

Name: _____ **Date:** _____

Directions: Name each picture below. Write the missing *p*'s. Then color the pictures.

1.

_____

pumpkin

2.

_____

ig

3.

_____

arrot

4.

_____

ie

Name: _____ **Date:** _____

Directions: Trace and write the letter *Qq*.

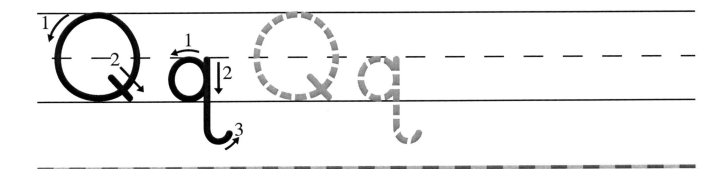

Directions: Find and color all of the *q*'s.

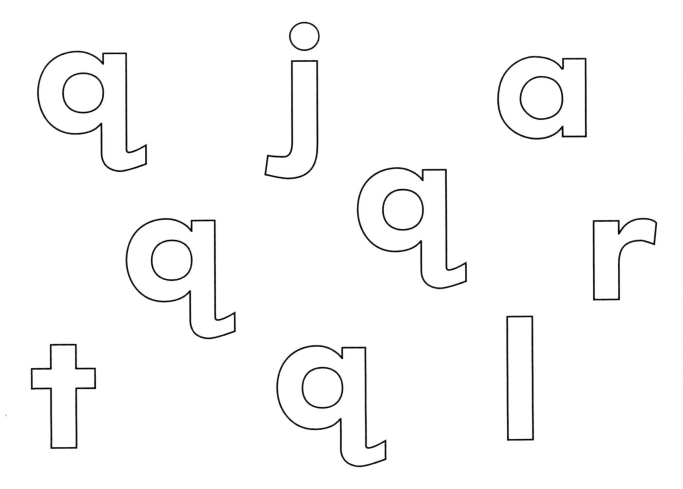

Primary Sound *q*

Name: _____ **Date:** _____

Directions: Write the missing *q*'s. Then color the pictures.

1.

quilt

2.

ueen

3.

uail

4.

uarter

Name: _____ **Date:** _____

Directions: Trace and write the letter *Rr*.

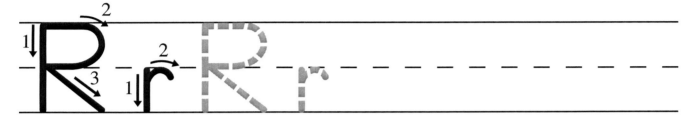

Directions: Name each picture below. Follow the *r* pictures to find your way out of the maze.

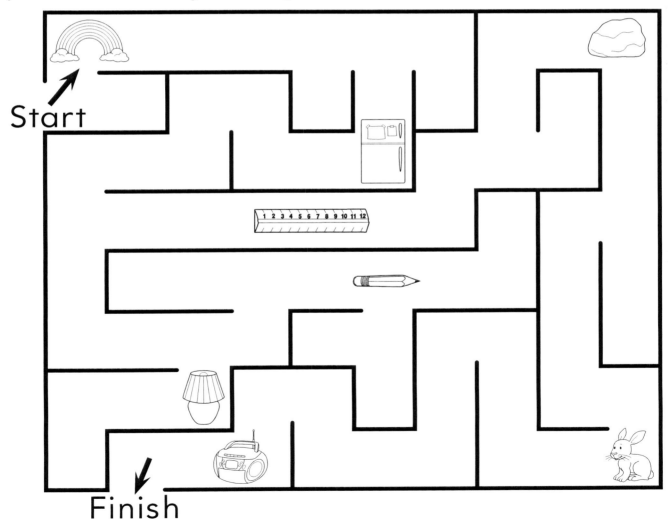

Primary Sound *r*

Name: _____ **Date:** _____

Directions: Name each picture below. Write the missing *r*'s. Then color the pictures.

1. rabbit

2. ___ock

3. ___ainbow

4. ___adio

Name: _____ **Date:** _____

Directions: Trace and write the letter *Ss*.

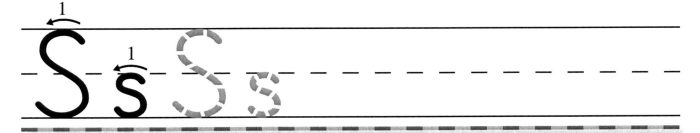

Directions: Follow the snail trail around the track.
Trace each *s* along the way.

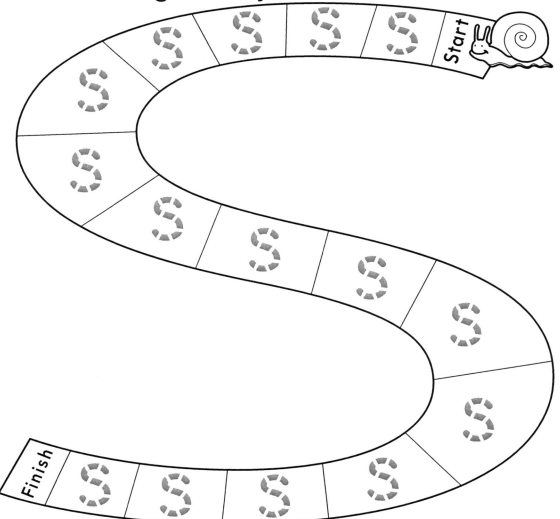

Primary Sound *s*

Name: _____ **Date:** _____

Directions: Look at the picture. Color the things that begin with *s*.

Primary Sound *t*

Name: _____ **Date:** _____

Directions: Trace and write the letter *Tt*.

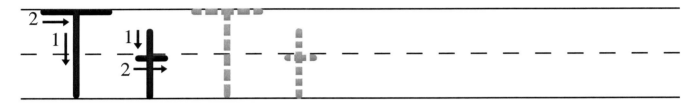

Directions: Name each picture below. Draw a line to match the pictures that go together.

Primary Sound *t*

Name: _____ **Date:** _____

Directions: Look at the letters below. Find and color the boxes that have *t*'s in them. What did you make?

f	l	t	m	y
v	w	t	x	z
h	t	t	t	d
k	m	t	g	l
s	n	t	o	o
r	j	t	p	k

Directions: Name each picture below. Circle the pictures that begin with *t*.

Name: _____ **Date:** _____

Directions: Trace and write the letter *Uu*.

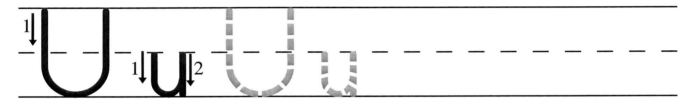

Directions: Find and color all of the *u*'s.

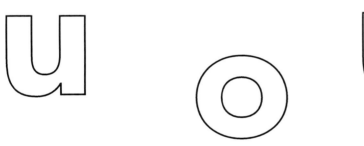

Primary Sound *u*

Name: _____ **Date:** _____

Directions: Write the missing *u*'s. Color the pictures.

1.  c ___ p	2.  c ___ b
3.  b ___ g	4.  b ___ s

Name: _____ **Date:** _____

Directions: Trace and write the letter *Vv*.

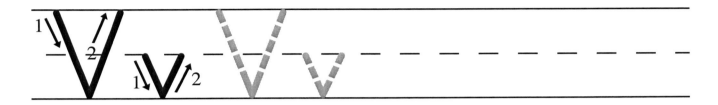

Directions: Find and color all of the *v*'s.

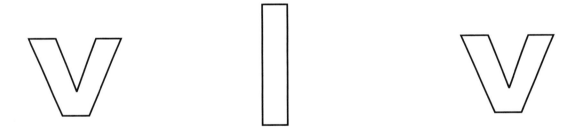

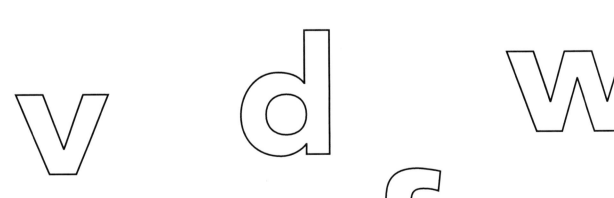

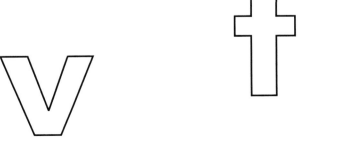

Primary Sound *v*

Name: _____ **Date:** _____

Directions: Write the missing *v*'s. Color the pictures.

1.  _____ vacuum	2.  _____ an
3.  _____ est	4. 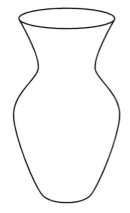 _____ ase

Name: _____ **Date:** _____

Directions: Trace and write the letter *Ww*.

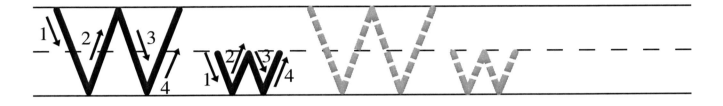

Directions: Color the puzzle pieces with *w*'s on them.

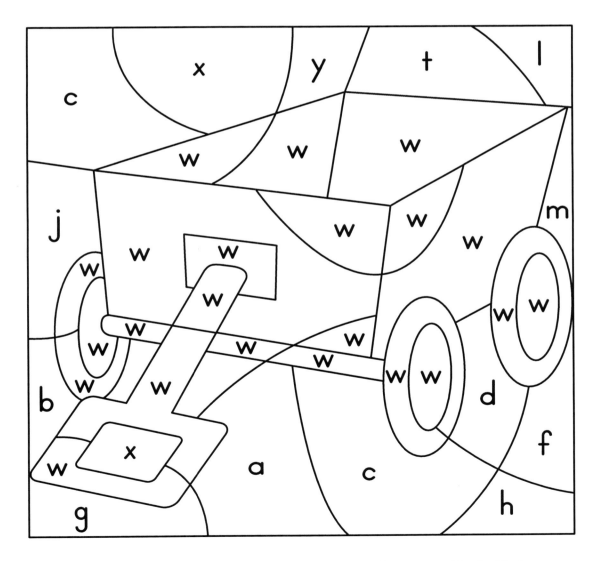

Primary Sound *w*

Name: _____ **Date:** _____

Directions: Name each picture below. Write the missing *w*'s. Then color the pictures.

1. waiter	2. __eb
3. __atch	4. __allet
5. __affle	6. __and

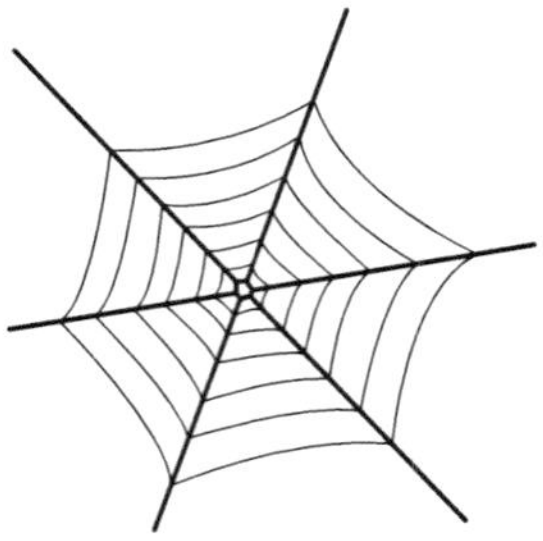

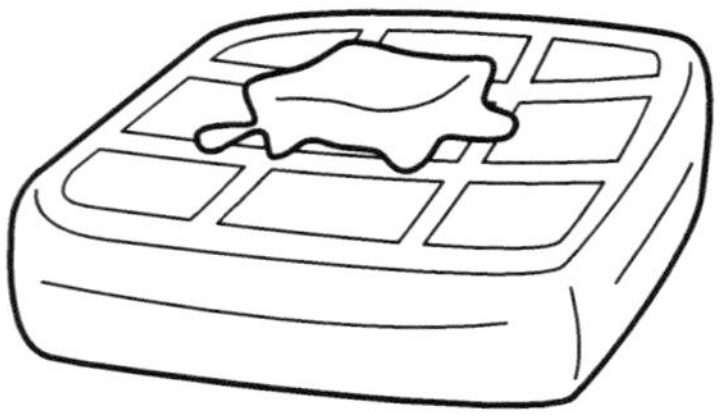

Name: _____ **Date:** _____

Directions: Trace and write the letter *Xx*.

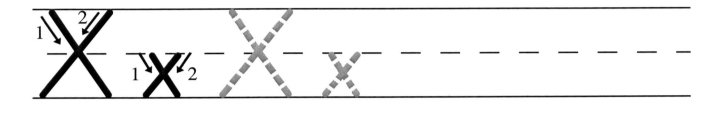

Directions: Find and color all of the *x*'s.

   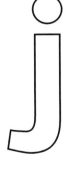

Primary Sound x

Name: _____ **Date:** _____

Directions: Write the missing x's. Color the pictures.

1.

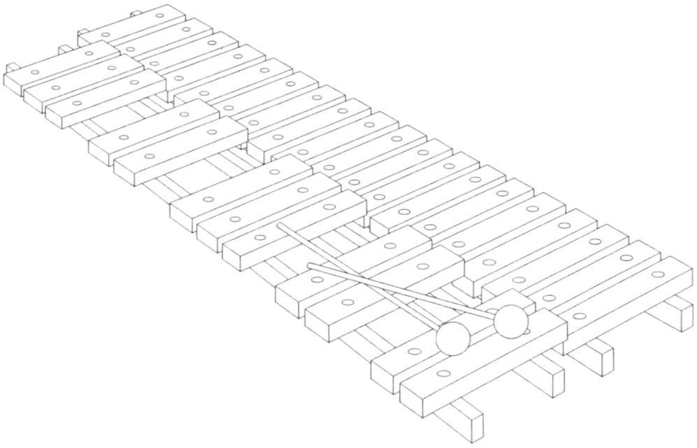

xylophone

2.

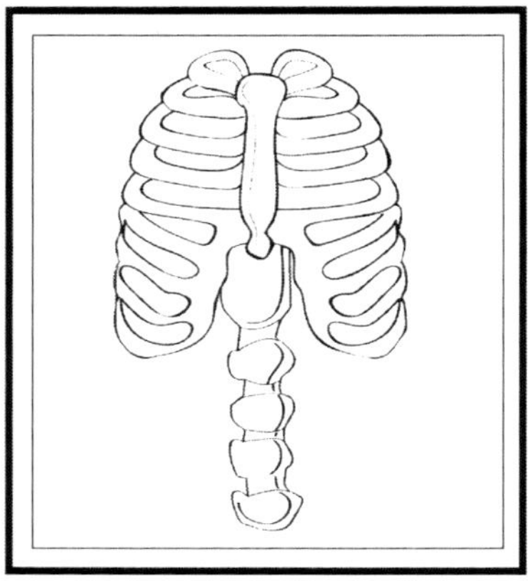

___ray

Name: _____ **Date:** _____

Directions: Trace and write the letter _Yy_.

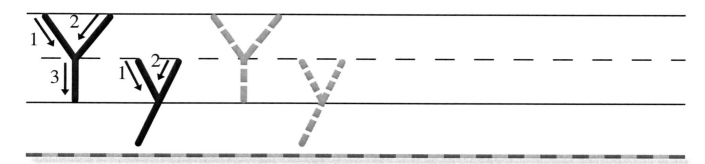

Directions: Find and color all of the _y_'s.

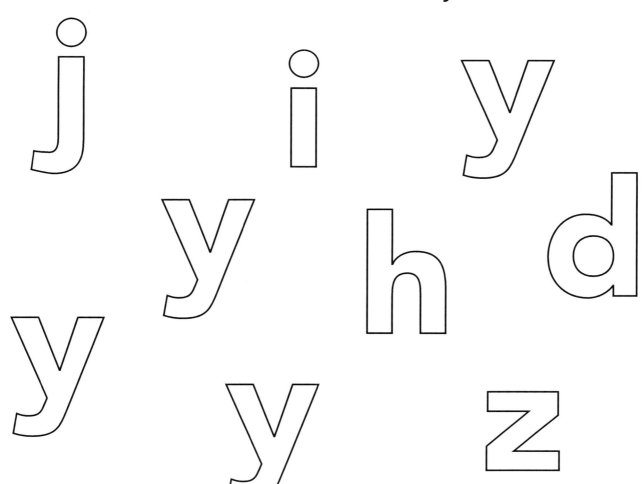

Primary Sound *y*

Name: _____ **Date:** _____

Directions: Write the missing *y*'s. Then color the pictures.

1. 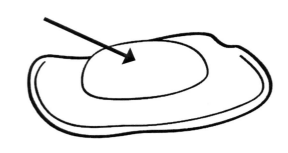 ____ yolk	2.  ____ ak
3.  ____ awn	4.  ____ ogurt

Name: _____ **Date:** _____

Directions: Trace and write the letter *Zz*.

Directions: Find and color all of the *z*'s.

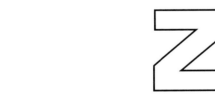

Primary Sound z

Name: _____ **Date:** _____

Directions: Write the missing z's. Then color the pictures.

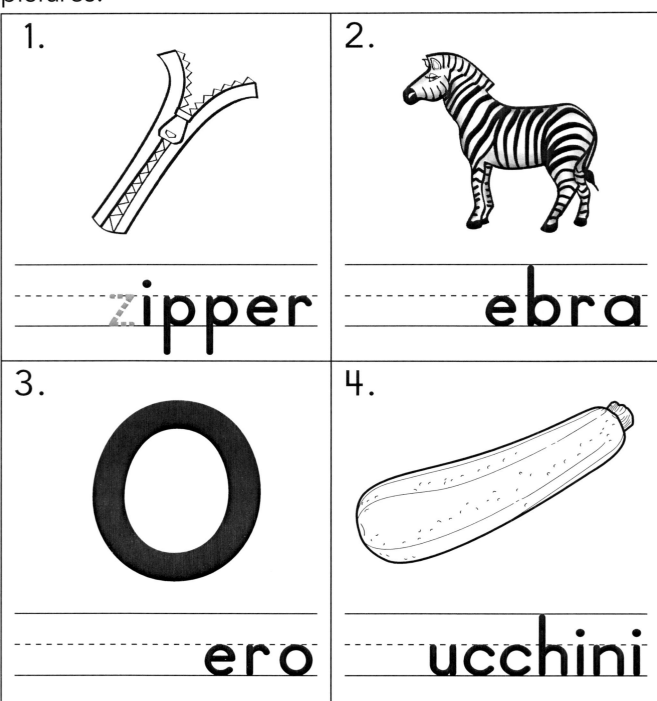

1.

_____
z̲ipper

2.

_____
____ebra

3.

_____
____ero

4.

_____
____ucchini

Name: _____ **Date:** _____

Directions: Circle the pictures with the long *a* sound.

1.	2.
3.	4.
5.	6.

Vowel Focus

Name: _____**Date:** _____

Directions: Name each picture below. Circle *short* or *long* for the vowel sound it makes.

1.  short long	2.  short long
3. 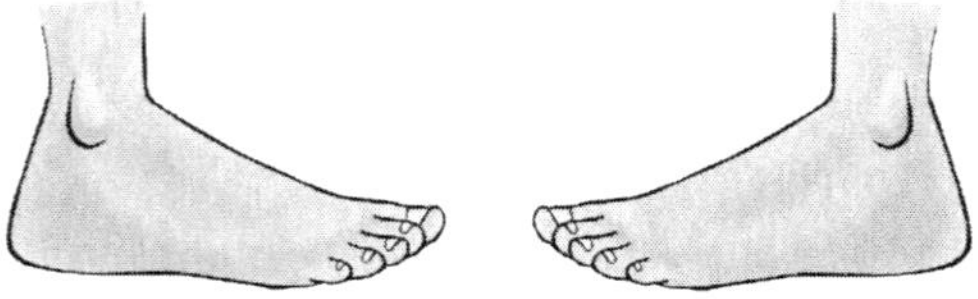 short long	4.  short long
5.  short long	6.  short long

Name: _____ **Date:** _____

Directions: Mike likes things that have the long *i* sound. Say the name of each picture. Draw lines from the pictures with the long *i* sound to Mike.

Vowel Focus

Name: _____ **Date:** _____

Directions: Name each picture below. Fill in the *short* or *long* bubble for the vowel sound it makes.

1. 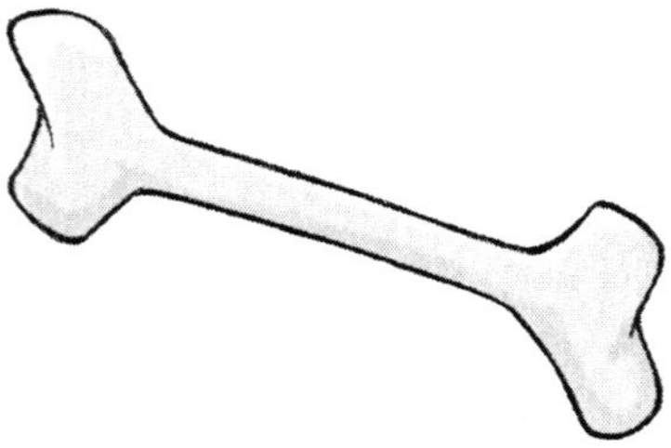 ◯ short ◯ long	2. 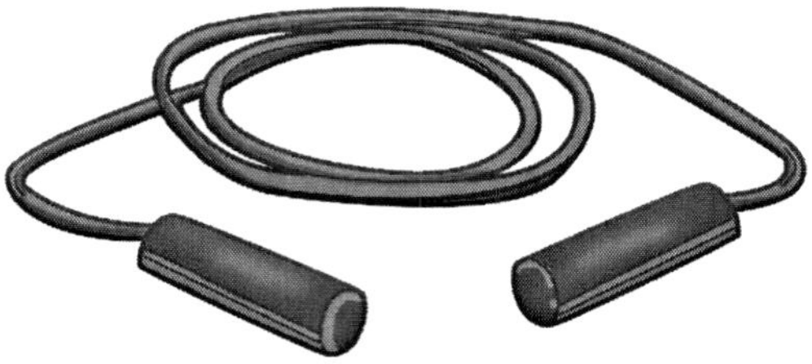 ◯ short ◯ long
3. 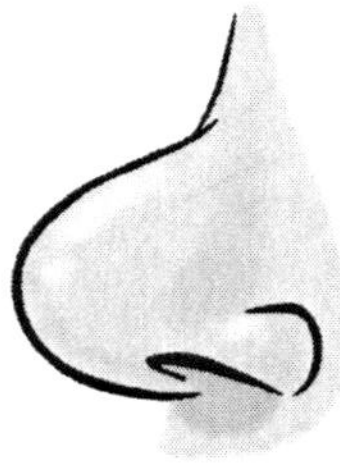 ◯ short ◯ long	4.  ◯ short ◯ long
5.  ◯ short ◯ long	6.  ◯ short ◯ long

Name: _____ **Date:** _____

Directions: Circle the picture if the word has the long *u* sound. Put an *X* on the picture if the word has the short *u* sound.

1.	2.
3.	4.
5.	6.

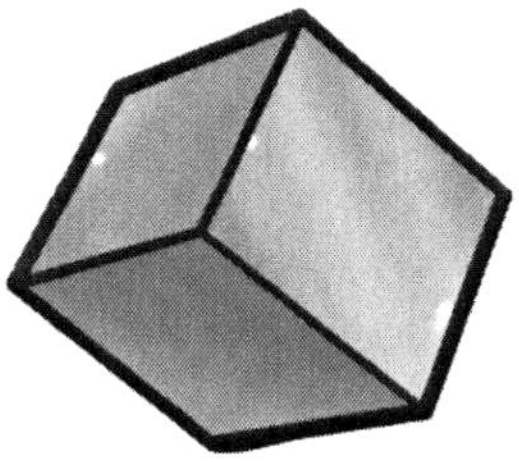

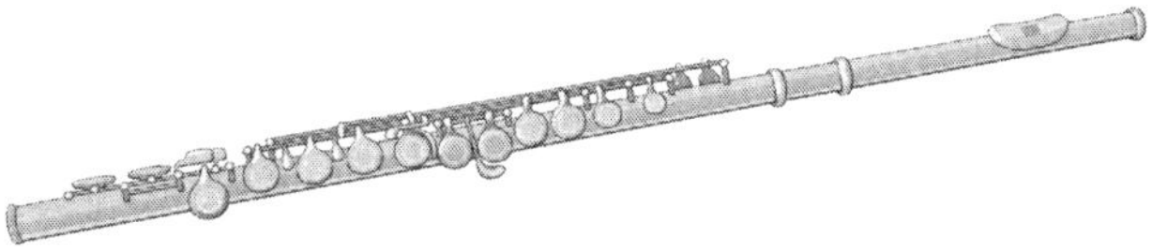

Vowel Focus

Name: _____ **Date:** _____

Directions: Name each picture below. Circle *short* or *long* for the vowel sound it makes.

1. short   long

2. short   long

3. short   long

4. short   long

5. short   long

6. short   long

Vowel Focus

Name: _____ **Date:** _____

Directions: Name each picture below. Circle the vowel sound you hear.

1.

a e i o u

2.

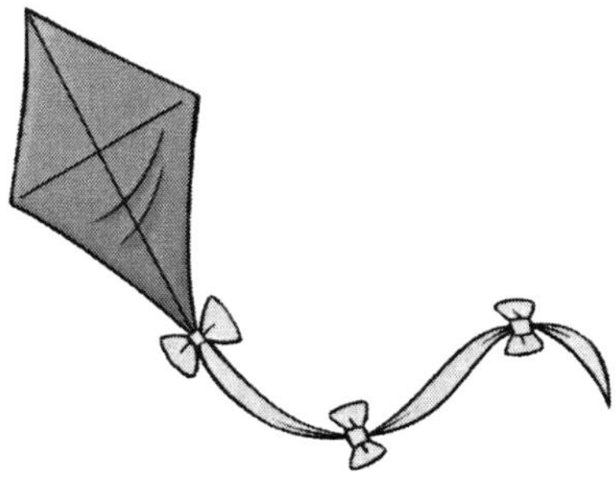

a e i o u

3.

a e i o u

4.

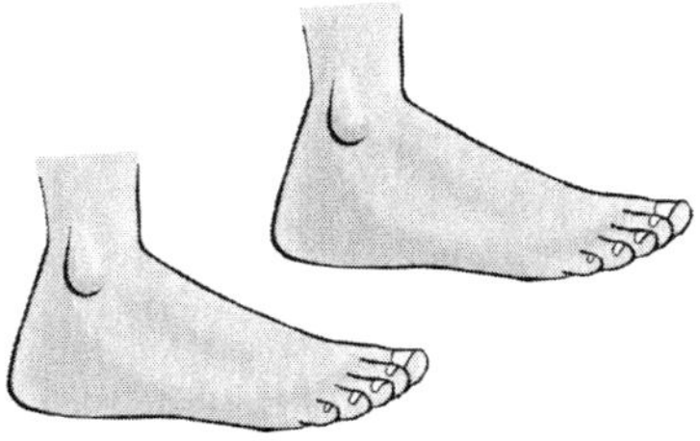

a e i o u

5.

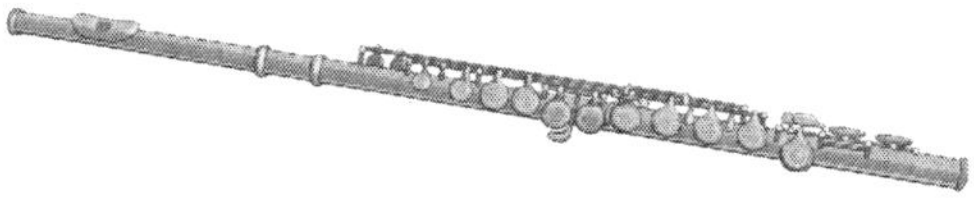

a e i o u

6.

a e i o u

Vowel Focus

Name: _____ **Date:** _____

Directions: Name each picture below. Circle the vowel sound you hear.

1.

a e i o u

2.

a e i o u

3.

a e i o u

4.

a e i o u

5.

a e i o u

6.

a e i o u

Name: _____ **Date:** _____

Directions: Circle the word for each picture.

1. 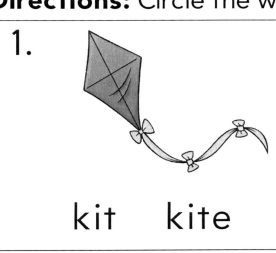 kit kite	2. 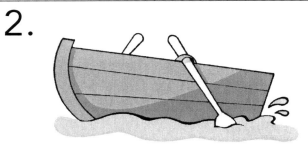 bot boat
3. 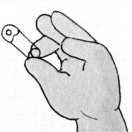 pin pine	4.  tub tube
5.  cap cape	6.  hop hope

Vowel Focus

Name: _____ **Date:** _____

Directions: Circle the words that rhyme.

1.	lake rake tap take
2.	zone hog cone lone
3. **5**	tip dive line pine
4.	fame can same tame
5.	role mole pole hop
6.	hire wire tip tire

Name: _____ **Date:** _____

Directions: Draw lines to match the sight words.

1. the   my

2. my   the

Directions: Write the missing sight words.

3. the car

4. cap

5. car

6. cap

Sight Words

Name: _____ **Date:** _____

Directions: Write each sight word two times.

of	to

Directions: Draw lines to match the words that go together.

of	**of**
to	**to**
to	of
of	to

Name: _____ **Date:** _____

Directions: Read the sentences. Circle *yes* or *no*.

1. Is it a cat?  yes no	2. Is it a fan? 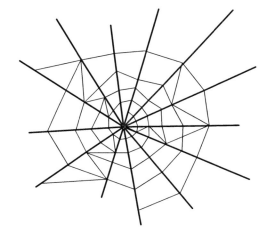 yes no
3. Is it a bed?  yes no	4. Is it a mop?  yes no

Sight Words

Name: _____ **Date:** _____

Directions: Trace the words. Then write the words.

1. he   he   _____

2. she   she   _____

Directions: Write the missing sight words.

3. _she_ draws

4. _____ sleeps

5. _____ runs

6. _____ eats

Name: _____ **Date:** _____

Directions: Write each sight word two times.

1. **was** ‾‾‾‾‾‾‾‾‾‾‾‾‾‾‾‾‾‾‾ ‾‾‾‾‾‾‾‾‾‾‾‾‾‾‾‾‾

2. **saw** ‾‾‾‾‾‾‾‾‾‾‾‾‾‾‾‾‾‾‾ ‾‾‾‾‾‾‾‾‾‾‾‾‾‾‾‾‾

Directions: Find and circle the words *was* and *saw*.

a w s a w a

s a s w a s

a w a s w a

s a w a s w

Sight Words

Name: _____**Date:** _____

Directions: Draw lines to match the sight words.

1. **do**　　　　　　　**you**

2. you　　　　　　　**do**

Directions: Answer the questions *yes* or *no*.

3.  Do you yell? _____ - - - - - - - - - - - - _____	4.  Do you sit? _____ - - - - - - - - - - - - _____
5.  Do you run? _____ - - - - - - - - - - - - _____	6.  Do you sing? _____ - - - - - - - - - - - - _____

Name: _____ **Date:** _____

Directions: Read the two words in each box. Circle the word that matches the picture. Then write the word in the blank.

1. men ⟨mat⟩		_mat_
2. hat hug		
3. cut cat		
4. bat hat		
5. rip rat		

Similarly Spelled

Name: _____ **Date:** _____

Directions: Read the words in the box. Choose a word to complete each sentence. Write the word in the blank.

bin   din   pin   ~~win~~

1. I can __win__.

2. I see a _____.

3. I hear the _____.

4. I see the _____.

Name: _____ **Date:** _____

Directions: Name each picture below. Then use the letters in the box to complete each word.

| h | l | r | -s- |

1.	 _____ s _____ **ip**
2.	 _____ _____ **ip**
3.	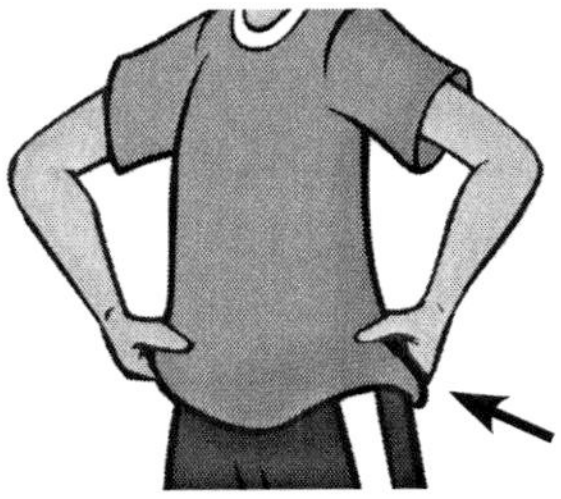 _____ _____ **ip**
4.	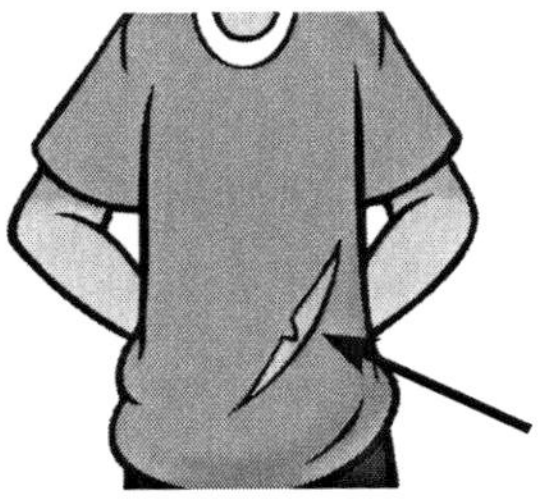 _____ _____ **ip**

Similarly Spelled

Name: _____ **Date:** _____

Directions: Read each sentence. Then read the words below it. Circle the correct word to complete each sentence. Write the word in the blank.

1. I have a _____pit_____.

   (pit)   pat

2. I got _____!

   bit   bat

3. I got a _____.

   hit   hat

4. I have a _____.

   mutt   mitt

5. Get the _____!

   cat   kit

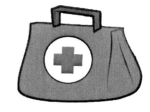

Similarly Spelled

Name: _____ **Date:** _____

Directions: Read the words under each picture. Draw an X on the pictures that do *not* have the *-op* sound.

mop

rip

pot

top

hop

bop

pop

hot

Similarly Spelled

Name: _____ **Date:** _____

Directions: Choose a word that matches the art in each sentence. Write the word in the blank.

| hen   men   pen   ten |

1. I see a ___hen___.

2. I see a _____.

3. I see _____ hens!

4. I see _____ in

the pen.

Name: _____ **Date:** _____

Directions: Name each picture below. Write the missing letters in the blank.

1. ru_g_

2. __ ug

3. h___

4. mu__

5. __ ug

Similarly Spelled

Name: _____ **Date:** _____

Directions: Name each picture below. Then look at the letters in the box. Choose a letter for each word to match the pictures.

h	m	c	n

1.	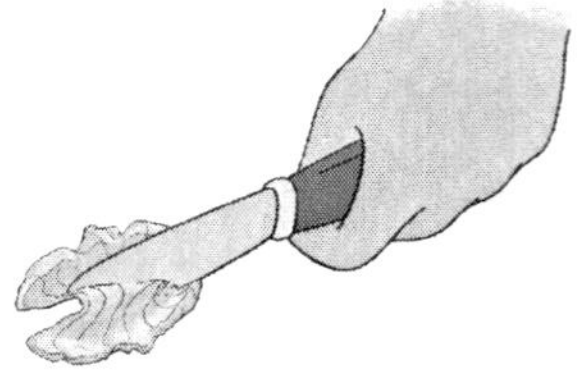 ___ ut
2.	 ___ utt
3.	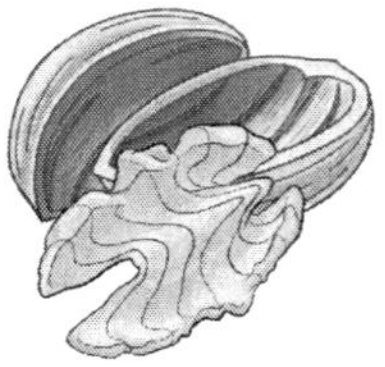 ___ ut
4.	 ___ ut

Chall, Jeanne S. 1995. *Learning to read: The great debate*, 3rd ed. Orlando: Harcourt Brace.

Cook, Vivian. 2004. *Accomodating brocolli in the cemetary: Or, why can't anybody spell?* New York: Touchstone.

Fry, Edward B., and Jacqueline E. Kress. 2006. *The reading teacher's book of lists*, 5th ed. San Francisco: Jossey-Bass.

Griffith, Priscilla L., and Mary W. Olson. 1992. Phonemic awareness helps beginning readers break the code. *The Reading Teacher*, 45: 516–523.

Juel, C. 1988. Learning to read and write: A longitudinal study of 54 children from first to fourth grades. *Journal of Educational Psychology*, 78: 243–255.

Lomax, Richels G., and Lomax M. McGee. 1987. Young children's concepts about print and meaning: Toward a model of reading acquisition. *Reading Research Quarterly*, 22: 237–256.

National Governors Association Center for Best Practices and Council of Chief State School Officers. 2010. Common core standards. http://corestandards.org/the-standards.

National Reading Panel. 2000. *Report of the National Reading Panel: Teaching children to read*. Washington, DC: Donald N. Langenberg, chair.

Tunmer, William E., and Richard A. Nesdale. 1985. Phonemic segmentation skill and beginning reading. *Journal of Educational Psychology*, 77: 417–427.

Answer Key

page 11

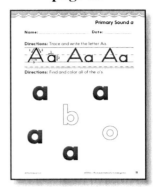

page 15

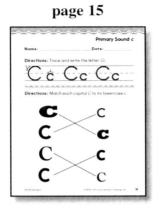

page 19

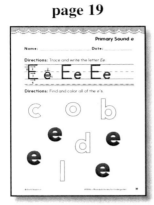

page 12

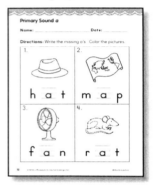

page 16

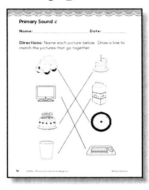

page 20

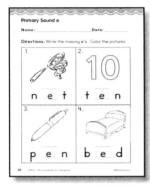

page 13

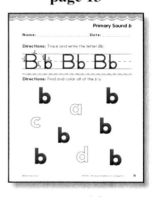

page 17

page 21

page 14

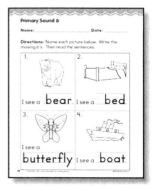

page 18

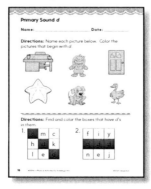

page 23

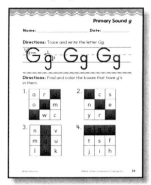

page 27

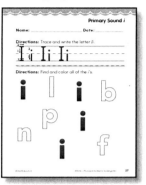

page 31

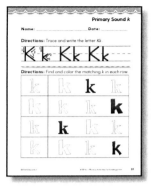

page 24

page 28

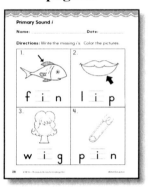

page 32

page 25

page 29

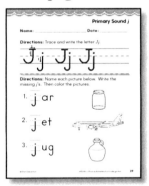

page 33

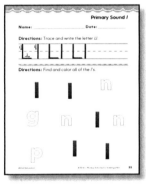

page 26

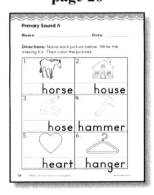

page 30

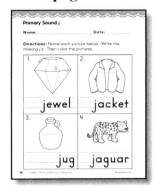

page 34

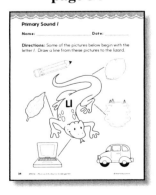

Answer Key (cont.)

page 35

page 36

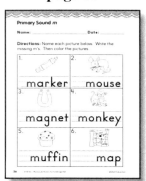

page 37

page 38

page 39

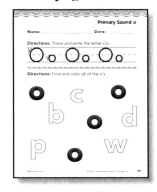

page 40

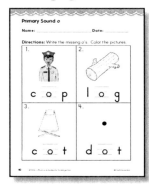

page 41

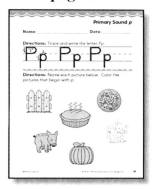

page 42

page 43

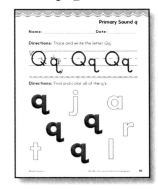

page 44

page 45

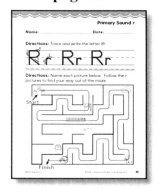

page 46

page 47

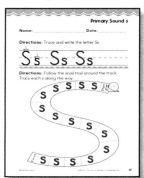

page 51

page 55

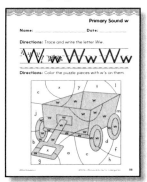

page 48

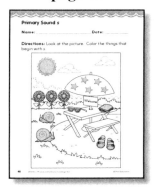

page 52

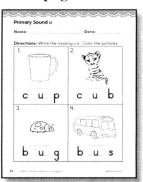

page 56

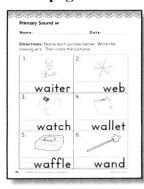

page 49

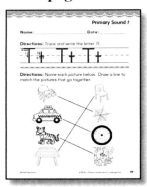

page 53

page 57

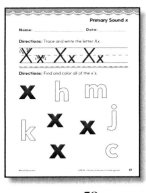

page 50

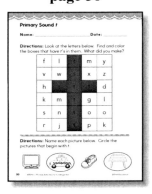

page 54

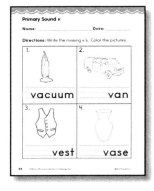

page 58

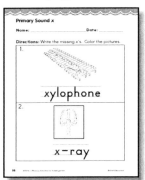

Answer Key *(cont.)*

page 59

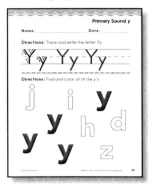

page 63

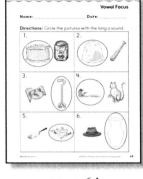

page 67

page 60

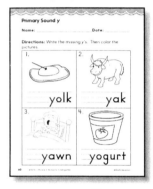

page 64

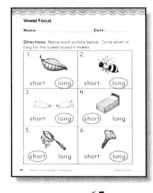

page 68

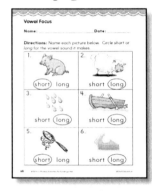

page 61

page 65

page 69

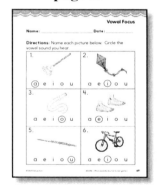

page 62

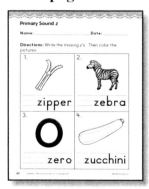

page 66

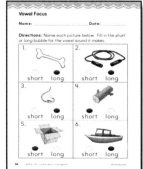

page 70

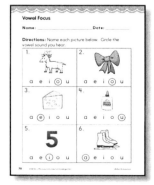

page 71

page 75

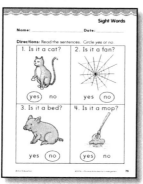

page 79

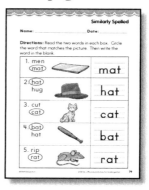

page 72

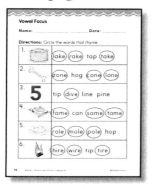

page 76

page 80

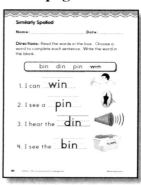

page 73

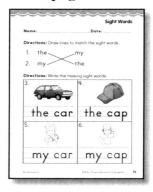

page 77

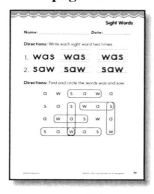

page 81

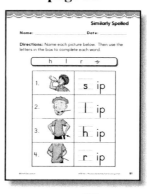

page 74

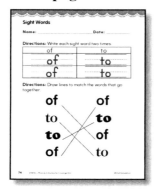

page 78

page 82

page 83

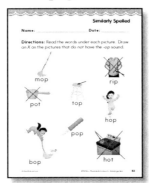

page 86

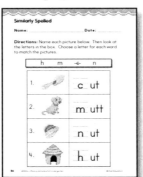

page 84

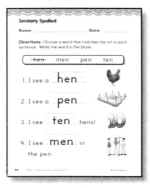

page 85

Page	Filename
11	page11.pdf
12	page12.pdf
13	page13.pdf
14	page14.pdf
15	page15.pdf
16	page16.pdf
17	page17.pdf
18	page18.pdf
19	page19.pdf
20	page20.pdf
21	page21.pdf
22	page22.pdf
23	page23.pdf
24	page24.pdf
25	page25.pdf
26	page26.pdf
27	page27.pdf
28	page28.pdf
29	page29.pdf
30	page30.pdf
31	page31.pdf
32	page32.pdf
33	page33.pdf
34	page34.pdf
35	page35.pdf
36	page36.pdf
37	page37.pdf
38	page38.pdf
39	page39.pdf
40	page40.pdf
41	page41.pdf
42	page42.pdf
43	page43.pdf
44	page44.pdf
45	page45.pdf
46	page46.pdf
47	page47.pdf
48	page48.pdf
49	page49.pdf

Page	Filename
50	page50.pdf
51	page51.pdf
52	page52.pdf
53	page53.pdf
54	page54.pdf
55	page55.pdf
56	page56.pdf
57	page57.pdf
58	page58.pdf
59	page59.pdf
60	page60.pdf
61	page61.pdf
62	page62.pdf
63	page63.pdf
64	page64.pdf
65	page65.pdf
66	page66.pdf
67	page67.pdf
68	page68.pdf
69	page69.pdf
70	page70.pdf
71	page71.pdf
72	page72.pdf
73	page73.pdf
74	page74.pdf
75	page75.pdf
76	page76.pdf
77	page77.pdf
78	page78.pdf
79	page79.pdf
80	page80.pdf
81	page81.pdf
82	page82.pdf
83	page83.pdf
84	page84.pdf
85	page85.pdf
86	page86.pdf

Notes